In Earthlight

BOOKS BY JONATHAN GRIFFIN

Politics

Britain's Air Policy, Victor Gollancz, 1935
Alternative to Rearmament, Macmillan, 1936
Glasshouses and Modern War, Chatto and Windus, 1938
Lost Liberty: The Ordeal of the Czechs (with Joan Griffin), Chatto and
   Windus, 1936

Poetry

The Hidden King (a verse trilogy), Secker & Warburg, 1955
The Rebirth of Pride, Secker & Warburg, 1957
The Oath and other poems, Giles Gordon, 1962
In Time of Crowding, Brookside Press, 1975
In this Transparent Forest, Green River Press, 1977
Outsing the Howling, Permanent Press, 1979
The Fact of Music, The Menard Press, 1980
Commonsense of the Senses, The Menard Press, 1983
Collected Poems (Vols 1 & 2), National Poetry Foundation, Maine,
   1989 & 1990

Poetry Translations

The Journals of Pierre Menard no. 4 (Griffin issue), October 1969
Von Kleist: *The Prince of Homburg*, Plays of the Year, Elek 1969 (now
   available from Menard)
Fernando Pessoa, I - IV, Carcanet 1971
Fernando Pessoa: *Selected Poems*, Penguin Books, 1974
   (2nd expanded edition, 1982)
René Char: *Poems* (trs JG or M-A Caws), Princeton U. P., 1976
Camoens: *Gentle Spirit*, The Menard Press, 1976
Jorge de Sena: *Sobra Esta Praia*, Inklings (Santa Barbara), 1979
Jean Mambrino: *The Inner Gold*, The Menard Press, 1979
Jean Mambrino: *Glade*, Enitharmon Press, 1986
Fernando Pessoa: *Message*, Menard/Kings, 1992
Rimbaud: *Complete Poems in Verse and Prose* (unpublished)

Other Translations

Montherlant (8 plays), de Gaulle, Giono, Kazantzakis, Gary, Rostand,
Huyghe, Lilar, Vallier, Barrault, Bresson

On Jonathan Griffin

Sage Eye: The Aesthetic Passion of Jonathan Griffin,
   edited by Anthony Rudolf, Menard/Kings 1992

IN EARTHLIGHT
Selected Poems
Jonathan Griffin

Edited by Jonathan Delamont
Foreword by Carl Rakosi

The Menard Press
London

In Earthlight

Selected Poems by Jonathan Griffin

Edited by Jonathan Delamont

© 1995 The Menard Press

Frontispiece specially created for this book by Julia Farrer
Cover design by Audrey Jones
Design, setting and camera ready copy by Lijna Minnet

Acknowledgements to:The National Poetry Foundation,
University of Maine, Maine 04469, who published Jonathan
Griffin's *Collected Poems* Vol.1 (1989) and Vol. 2 (1990)

Representation and distribution in UK:
Central Books (Troika)
99 Wallis Road, Hackney Wick, London E9 5LN
Tel: 0181-986 4854

Distribution in the rest of the world apart from North America:
Central Books

Distribution in North America:
SPD Inc
1814 San Pablo Avenue, Berkeley CA 94702 USA

ISBN: 1-874320-12-8

The Menard Press
8 The Oaks
Woodside Avenue
London N12 8AR
Tel: 0181-446 5571

Printed and bound by
Arc & Throstle Press
Todmorden, Lancashire

Ill fares the land, to hastening ills a prey,
Where wealth accumulates, and men decay;
Princes and lords may flourish or may fade;
A breath can make them, as a breath has made:
But a bold peasantry, their country's pride,
When once destroy'd, can never be supplied.
A time there was, ere England's griefs began,
When every rood of ground maintained its man;
For him light labour spread her wholesome store,
Just gave what life required, but gave no more:
His best companions, innocence and health,
And his best riches, ignorance of wealth.
But times are altered; trade's unfeeling train
Usurp the land and dispossess the swain;
Along the lawn, where scattered hamlets rose,
Unwieldy wealth, and cumbrous pomp repose;
And every want to opulence allied,
And every pang that folly pays to pride.

Oliver Goldsmith
from *The Deserted Village* 1770

FOREWORD

Carl Rakosi

It would be presumptuous for an American poet to introduce an English poet to English readers. They are perfectly capable of appraising Jonathan Griffin accurately themselves. Some discriminating readers have, but sometimes local circumstances stand in the way. Hence a word from an outsider.

When I first began to read Jonathan Griffin, I couldn't help noticing that nowhere in his work did I find any fudging. Even his clashes with God were met head-on. It was equally remarkable that despite the scope and seriousness of his subject matter, there was no padding. That puts him in a special class, which he was much too modest to claim for himself but which I can claim for him. Nor was there any ornamentation, no dressing up for effect or rhetoric. No effort, in short, to enhance what he has to say by metaphor or to develop a mystery about his subject matter. And no literary games (what a relief!). He is too honest for that. His subject matter is powerful enough to stand on its own; plus, he has the literary skill to make it suffice.

This power comes partly from the fact that he is deeply philosophical, concerned with the great concerns of mankind. In his poems he is heard as if talking to himself about them, not trying to convince anyone but calling out in his distress like Job. He has the intellect to carry this off so that it never seems grandiose. At bottom he is grave and serious but not portentous. And sometimes he is comical, as in the lines from his poem, *Wonders Of The Shore*: "It would be fun to own/a collection of senior civil servants." Throughout he is clear and straightforward. His use of spacing gives his poems a particularly clean look on the page and is part of their meaning. What is not so easily noticed is that this thought perfectly matches his language, which he uses with the utmost economy.

One other thing. Often the language is fractured but not

disjunct or disorderly. This might turn some readers off whose pleasure in poetry is based on the flow and cadence of natural sentences but if one can take a chance on something different, there is much to be said for fracturing. It pinpoints ideas and images better. Also it is the way the mind works, in spurts, and catches thoughts on the fly. In that sense it is quite natural, more natural than the literary sentence. As a consequence, there is a preponderance of nouns, as in Oppen's poetry, which goes with the preponderance of ideas in his work. From this one can say that Jonathan Griffin is more interested in what he has to say than in the pleasure of hearing himself say it in literary language.

As I read him, he is a big, serious poet, with an excellent ear and powers of perception and discretion. In the two volumes of his *Collected Poems* published in America by the National Poetry Foundation at the University of Maine there are over 800 pages of poetry. This smaller collection makes it easier for the English reader to discover Jonathan Griffin. I wish it a happy voyage.

JONATHAN GRIFFIN
1908 - 1990

Jonathan Delamont

In the last thirty years there has been no miscarriage of poetic justice more serious yet more understandable than the inattention given to the poetry of Jonathan Griffin. Serious, because he was a master-poet with incontrovertibly urgent and important things to say; and understandable, because the poems are so prescient – forward-looking, in the undebased sense of the term – that until very recently they would have been most unlikely to have attracted much of the deadly serious notice which they merit. This is for a whole raft of reasons, all connected with the complacent ostrichism of the typical native of the twentieth century, its literati not excluded: whose sins of omission are even now beginning to be visited upon his or her own children, and children's children, with a vengeance none the less cruel for being unlooked-for and unmeant. For those of us who are going to have to live with the results, Jonathan Griffin is and is going to be one of the few late-twentieth-century poets with anything of relevance to say to us.

Griffin fulfilled his ambition 'to live long/to die young': by contrast, ninety-nine out of a hundred 'contemporary poets', old and young, seem even now to be pursuing an agenda which, like the proverbial generals, commits them to a fight for aesthetic wars long since won and lost, on behalf of long obsolete futures. But then it is perhaps more depressing than surprising that the 'progressive' literary sense-organs are no better than any conservative's rose-tinted spectacles in their common tendency to filter out all perception that does not fall within a pre-set wave-band width of preconception, according to which *diktat* one is free to play with the buttons provided, but not, emphatically not, with the tuning of the mind-set itself.

One such unquestioned preconception, widely-held by poet/

critics who should know better, is that 'Green poetry' is perforce polemical and shallow, a trendy obsession of the younger poet-aspirant not yet purged of all such nonsense by a more mature judgment: as though world economic concerns, upon which ride all hopes for any vestige of a leisured and cultured existence (as demanded, more or less as of right, by lovers of literature no less than others) were not utterly dependent upon global ecological concerns; so that it could with justice be counter-argued that any poetry which is *not* in some real sense engaged with ecological concerns cannot be considered 'contemporary' by any coldly realistic critical test.

To the tiresome refrain, still to be heard like a nervous litany among metropolitan critics, over and over reassuring themselves that 'green politics' are a trendy and recent aberration in literature, the answer of course is that this is nonsense, as witnessed-to by the extract from Goldsmith's *'Deserted Village'*, chosen for the flyleaf for just this reason. Goldsmith's familiar and self-evidently durable words belie the assertion that 'Green Poetry' is necessarily shallow and ephemeral, even when it long outlasts the issue that prompted it into being. If anything, their continued accuracy in pin-pointing the causes and consequences of pseudo-progress increases their chilling impact, as we reflect how nothing has changed since his day except in the speed and scale at which we can destroy wild, semi-wild, and rural 'backwardness' in order to conflate the runaway vainglories of the nervous metropolis: hopelessly failing to contain itself, sacrificing the victims of its own success one by one like a Wild West locomotive burning its own carriages in order to continue down the same one track, headlong in flight from the fate that it has provoked. It ought to be obvious to everyone by now that now as never before *all* global politics are 'green', concerned with *Lebensraum*; too many people chasing too little of everything. The only undiscovered continent that remains is outer space, and even the richest nations are in no fit state to organise such an expansion. 'Gaian' theorist James Lovelock's upbeat plans for 'The Greening of Mars' are generations away from attainment: meanwhile, we are running out of time, and there is nowhere for anyone to escape to. The technological fantasies of O'Neill, Dyson, Zebrowski and their like are probably further off now than when they were proposed; and even if this were not so it would not alter the fact that civilised human continuance on our planet of origin is bound to involve strict ecological management requiring political decisions which are stern to the point of harshness, and realistic as to the inescapability of the second law of thermodynamics in a fashion utterly at odds with the profligate expansionism of the last two centuries. If this is not undertaken and achieved by a liberal-pluralist society, then the task will perforce fall to a more authoritarian one: there will be no other choice. The reality is that 'progress' is governed by Parkinson's law, and amounts to the acceleration of rates of exhaustion of all our means of continued existence. Of all contemporary poems written in English, Griffin's nightmare scenarios are among the least dispensable or disposable or redundant: however unpalatable this may be, it needs to be faced by all cosmopolitans wherever they are and whatever they think they are doing.

In Griffin's poetry, his fear for the future and rage against the sacrilegious greed of the present is in any case validated as poetry by the high poetic standard in light of which these concerns acquire their true depth: in numinous, visionary lyrics the best of which stand comparison with anything by Vaughan, Hopkins, or, obliquely, Clare, and which root the urgent and temporal concern firmly in the timeless. A further, 'philosophical' strain then balances the two in a severely searching and self-searching attempt, in the poet's own words, to 'edge towards a philosophy of life valid now', both because and despite of a profoundly held 'agnostic' *un*knowing, an uncertain certainty or faith-in-faith arrived at through and after having faced and outfaced all the many heads of the late-modernist, absurdist Hydra: self-evasive irony, existential self-torture, mechanarchic fatalism, the formalism of art-for-artifice's sake, or, or, or. Griffin's poetry is a far more compelling instance of a call to seriousness than any conceivable lecture or sermon; we should have been reading him assiduously ever since the publication of *In Time of Crowding* (1974). That we were never seriously alerted that we should do so says more about the should-know-betters than it does about Griffin.

The style perfectly echoes these contents, too: few besides Jonathan Griffin have within themselves so naturally blended traditional English lyricism with the prosody of modernism, and this no doubt is because of the organic relationship of these styles with, on the one hand, roots in rural life and word-craft, back through the 'lyric poetry' (song-lyrics) of the Jacobeans to the folk-song and ballad-lyrics whose still current conventions were stabilised in the mediaeval period; and, on the other, with the clash and clangour of the urban/modern, its harshnesses of artificial light, its sudden shifts of mood and style, its always impending sense of menace and catastrophe. The musical equivalent of the efforts of this musical poet is probably most closely exemplified by the work of Sir Michael Tippett, where a variant upon the folk-song-inspired musical language put into circulation by Vaughan Williams meets a variant upon the hectic, polytonal restlessness of Stravinsky anywhere between *The Rite of Spring* and *Agon*, sometimes head-on. If Griffin had actually composed any music, Tippett's *Triple Concerto* (1979) would be a good, exactly contemporaneous guess as to how *The Fact of Music*, scored rather than written, might sound, considering the music in general and the slow movement in particular.

The bearer of crucially important yet unsettling tidings is not readily accepted; and even once accepted, such is our superstitious faith in our media of communication, we assume that the issue once aired has been taken to heart and in hand, whereas the cruel fact is that something like the reverse is more usual. As one example out of many, Griffin's poem *Gentle People* (p.30) could be considered as a worthy yet somehow quaint statement, old news; until we read Van Der Post's new last chapter in his revised and enlarged *Lost World of the Kalahari* (Chatto and Windus 1988) and realise that the literary success of a 'message' does nothing to guarantee the success of the cause: the machine grinds on regardless. Any issue once out of the news is taken to be out of sight, out of mind, ignorable and passé: which is one very good reason why it needs no literary apologist's attentions to excuse Griffin's practice of emphasising and re-emphasising the same key points despite the shiftless yet restless demand, from lowbrow and highbrow alike, to be entertained with an unending supply of novel diversions.

Here is a selection of some of Griffin's most arresting poems, arranged more or less as the poet chose to order them in his *Collected Poems* (National Poetry Foundation of America, 1989 – 1990). In preparing this book I have to thank my wife Lesley, for her material assistance, inexhaustible patience, and always constructive criticism; Anthony Rudolf and Kate Griffin, for trusting and entrusting me with the task; and Carl Rakosi, not only for his excellent and succinct foreword, but also for having insisted the two volume *Collected Poems* into existence while Griffin was still alive to oversee it. In consequence there were few poems to appraise which did not exist in definitive, published versions. These poems, from *"From Between Claws"* to *"From In"*, we included for the sake of completeness.

Finally, a word on Griffin's organisation of poems on the page. The 'Zen-like' quality of the use of caesurae and words and phrases left hanging in space is a device which can provoke impatience in the reader through its over-use in recent years by the unskilled and the unconscientious. But Griffin's use of spacing, like e.e. cummings', is nowhere deployed to conceal poverty of thought or diction. The spacing is a sort of *coup-de-grace* applied in final drafting process, which is why it seems effortless, natural, and 'right': and why Griffin's haiku-like short poems – eg. *Con Amore* – succeed where most neo-bardic attempts at imitating haiku in English fail so miserably. In English, the equivalent of haiku needs to be sensitively reinvented: and in this as in other aspects of his literary quality, Griffin is far more capable than most.

In 1982 Griffin himself wrote: "The lay-out of the poems is

not random: it contains a simple notation, useful in reading aloud. A line with 5 stresses starts fairly near the left hand edge of the page, one with 4 stresses further to the right, one with 3 the same distance further, and so on: a reader who is unsure how many stresses to make in a line has only to observe where it begins.

This system of indentation is maintained strictly. Some other (and normal) expression-marks, such as breaks in a line (its later part or parts placed lower than the preceding) or enlarged spaces between lines or between words, are also used, but freely as the poem has seemed to require."

To conclude. An art like Jonathan Griffin's is – to be fair to those prospective critics whom I have just been doing my best to disarm in advance – difficult to unravel and assess, because, steeped as he was in the aristocratic creative values of a genuine *haute culture*, I am quite sure that there could have been no more reluctant player of the role of Jeremiah than he. By instinct a celebrant of European humane culture's finest moments, he would undoubtedly have wished for happier times and a more joyous song to sing. The contents as against the title of a late poem, *Fear of Music*, illustrates the cultural divide between Griffin and the artistic boundary-hoppers of my own generation, media-wise and perhaps too much at ease with the quick fix shock tactics of performance art, art-rock music, and the like; compromise art forms of a type which, for all his cultivation of young friends, he could surely only have regarded as, at best, dissimulatory and therefore doomed. But this is precisely the point: a man of Griffin's sensibilities does not take to writing 'protest songs' without a compelling reason. The reason is there in the poems: the least we can all do now is to make up for lost time by reading them.

CONTENTS Page

I
1955 – 1975

Selections from The Hidden King
Selections from The Hidden King   3
World Affairs   6
To No-God in the Night   7
The Open   8
From Shame I Write   8
Moon Prayer   9
From Under Fall-out   10
Fourth of April, 1964   11
The Chalk Pit   11
Oak Mutter   12
Prayer in Time of Crowding   13
Winter Birds from Street Level   14
Wonders of the Shore   14
Room   15
Before Deposition   29
Gentle People   30
Social Contract   30
Not Sins and Glosses   31
To Carry, not Drown   31
To a Vandal   32
White off White   33
The Language   33
What is Left   34
How it Seems   35
The Tenant's Story   36
Bog   37
Nothing and Yet   38
Tongues   39
The Minds of the Next Men   40
The Out of Touch   40
The First Age of Love   41
Prophily   45
It Snowed in the Night   46
The Partition   47
Carol   47
Coastal Stretch   48

III
1984 – 1990   95

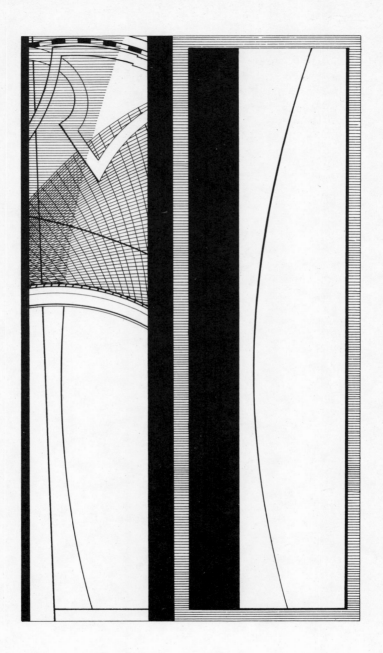

I

1955 - 1975

I   write for posterity Till lately
for some time one did not say that   Times
*   have changed*

Those of whom   we were posterity
*   left us room to live*

*   air*
*   unpoisoned seas*
*   fuel beyond our needs*
and many different monuments with faces

*   Our posterity are*
*   our victims one should face the stare*

*   In the halflifetime*
*   poems with the grace of shame.*

Original Preface, `In Time of Crowding'

The Hidden King, 'a poem for the stage in the form of a trilogy' (Secker and Warburg 1955; performed Edinburgh 1957) is Jonathan Griffin's earliest acknowledged work of poetry. It is in effect a long neo-Shakespearian tragedy written around the strange case of the 'reappearance' of Sebastian of Portugal in Venice in 1598, twenty years after his supposed death on crusade, much to the Machiavellian consternation of the grandees of the time. Griffin uses the tale as the basis for a dark meditation on the moral foundations of authority. Dividing critical opinion when performed, it appears to have suffered from the unpardonable *faux-pas* of being no longer fashionable; these soliloquy-samples hint at the literary quality of the text, which differs from its nearest equivalents, the verse-plays of Christopher Fry, in the severe discipline of the language, which concentrates not on mannerism but matter. Fry is at present undergoing reappraisal; *The Hidden King* merits no less, and could well be revived on radio, if nowhere else.

Man's freedom is to hang like a bell, free
To shudder, not to flee:
Tethered to testimony, the free man
Cannot escape: answer is all he can,
Answer each blow, out of the well of tone
That is his own.

*

The final training of a King is prison.
None of us loves his neighbour without prison.

I thought I loved my neighbour, having given
Proof of love. To have to leave
Loving God and turn again
To the craving of power, now seen clear, known
And feared and loathed; to waste our own
Soul for a hope (hopes are the shapes
Of vanity) the vaunting hope of saving
A people's soul (if indeed to be freed

Is to be made
Whole): I thought that was love.
Not enough!
A good man in prison is a man fallen among thieves
Set to sell thieves to thieves who keep alive
Stealing from thieves. He is immured with evil:
Evil men whom prison
Damns to the deep of evil.
My neighbour in the common prison
Filched the food of a stinking fool
Grown old in that cold hell – and laughs
And does the same again...
No blame, no hate.
That was my life's
Seventh moment of happiness...
The cold hell fills
The common prison of the wide horizon.
Thieves to love.

★

The sudden unfreshness of life:
Not a child, but a dwarf...

...In the sudden peace of loss
The useless fist falls loose...
If the eyes of the Baptist had seen Christ on the cross
If no mercy of murder had spared those desert ears
The last words, the silence, the tears,
The drumming of disgrace;
If, if, without
The clemency of Salome,
John's brain had thought out
God's doubt –
Or sallow Lazarus alone again:
When Lazarus, alone with dread

Of death the known, mourned for God dead...
Now I am lost in persecuted woods!
The woods, the belling woods are all cut down,
The soil itself sifted to a shifting dune!
The world is a dead woman – cold
Womb, still
Fertile – of worm.
Age within youth, despair under belief,
Sybilline diminution of each life!
Either kill and be killed
Or kill, kill and grow old.
Man – Man is not good
But is less bad than God,
Not having made the world.
So many things so well worth while:
The whole vile.
Age-abridging death, come and come soon!

★

There is no faith, except belief
In a cause, or loving:
Religion is relief
From believing.

...Birth into an evil world
Absolves the evil yet to be willed:
Nothing is holy but the inner
Humbling pride of honour.

...Most regal frugal act – abdication
Of majesty of the imagination;
Purging the world to be worthy to be called to
The common resurrection of resilience.

★

1955 - 1975

WORLD AFFAIRS

No man's duty is to do
more than he can? If that were true!
The choice to save or doom the race
faces us: when we face its face
we see each other, the unknown.

We measure farther than we feel
and, in between the figures, fall.
Each human particle escapes
into waves – the paths have gaps.
Nature controlled hurls in our teeth
trite matters of life and death.
We are alone and not alone.

> The small talk
> of the fall of all

TO NO-GOD IN THE NIGHT

To no-god in the night
what words ring right?

    Self-made ill,
I will be well: repent
    in art, giving
thanks to the living; turn
    what would pray
into praise: earn
    eyes to tell
worth that tells. A point
of honour shines still:
    to praise all pride
    that is clear-eyed.
        I will.

Speak.   Wait.   Because
pride has no need of echoes,
the words ring despite
the void heard in the night.

THE OPEN

Man out in the first
open
                on the high
seas next to the sky
deck-lonely man
                    to you star-recognition
                        offers
true bearings but no course no destination.

FROM SHAME I WRITE

The priests at the great house – almost the long
search had missed them – burst from their safe hole,
                cast out by their own smell.
            Rather the Question than a foul
            element, man breathing himself!

            Hunted, well hidden, poetry
            stifles out to honesty.
Honour is   a man caught by the lungs.

MOON PRAYER

Fairer than anything on earth   Earth! –
           whole
           holy
    heaven-blue Earth   shawled in white
       (sunside-of-cirrus fabric
       and cumulus-knuckled lacework
       perpetual apparition
       opening rose of the winds)
    Goddess!   diseased
                 perhaps to death

The white music   the light blue
     look so pure – who
'd imagine the russet and green markings
     swarm with the germ   Man
        (within the petals
     Allvandal Man   sacker
     even of Heavenrose
     motherfucker Man
     Nature Matricidal)?

Flowfair heavenly body – meaning
     of the dead dance – sick
        Goddess!   I pray
           for you
           May
       that peerless body
heave antibodies defeat Man

Airy Earth   mother of dolphins

FROM UNDER FALL-OUT

Should there be any history to go down to

deserve some name not FIRST AGE OF THE MEAN

Cleared of carving / cluttered with ads the clean
lines ape flight stay grounded   blocks   stunted
The fall-out of Man (by Man only stinted)
– the self-sump of the half-lives – silts between

By the victims to come (once men now many)
        the ivory towers   ride   haunted

Thou shalt not kill even a million men
not even intercontinentally
delete a city's children and then deal
a dole to again debase the human money

You – I – survivor therefore murderer
shall treat each life as though it still were rare

FOURTH OF APRIL, 1964

      This April afternoon
      I had need of a God

in the green meadow by brown Ken Wood
      prayed for a God to pray to
             to guard
             the seeding
of the early unfolded
                two Red
Admirals moving like dead leaves.

THE CHALK PIT

      Here   in rare shelter
    this drone of hushing in my head

It's the shells of the dead that roar for ever
answering sea –
          shells built out
                ring over
ring
    by the widening lives of the dead
      they sheltered and have shed.

OAK MUTTER

for Michael Schmidt

That year
the end of winter silence of our wood
was split. Shouts, chatter and more shouts. Then
the thudding, which I knew,
the toothed whine, which I knew
(axe and saw are sounds born in our blood
and caught before the first green curled green ears bud).
I understood.
Men.   These,
feared before heard, are the hunt cries of men –
the savage animal, enemy of trees,
hungry again . . .
Now I could hear
that hacking gnawing pack daily more near.

But one day silence. No, not silence, song;
and soon the loud birds, more
birds than ever before,
built on my boughs boldly and with quick peck
kept the sharp worms in check.
My listening leaves unfolded, they swilled long
dayfuls of light . . . The men did not come back.

Have not come back. Spring again. But birds few.
Our wood is quiet. That? that was my own,
that brittle creaking from the bough this one
thin, tailless squirrel scarcely has made sway.
No worm has come to fret my leaves, but they
budded yellow, seem not to want to swill
the long good light. Why do I feel so ill?
The light –

        The light, yes, is as usual.
Only something was wrong with the dew.

1965

PRAYER IN TIME OF CROWDING

I could use silence Could do with again
            genuine air youth air
breathed out by oaks or a hillside of heather
Not by engines making engines and men
and women men and women mere too many
            doomed because together
earth under a road – no worms stream there
no roots – the wheeltrack cagework endless pen

Background unmusic shuts round The growth-wither
traffic pounds on
                packs down
                        We are in our din
Could use
        a new power
                    to give and win
room
        silence
            seasons again
                            weather –
each I I in the thick under the each other
to generate the open from within

1964

WINTER BIRDS FROM STREET LEVEL

Now one can see the surface of the sky –
see, not far, the skin of that clear lake, by
the catspaws of a wind ruffling the sky:
dark-showing it, the flexing preparations
          for the migrations.

Those figures still the deep of the mind, make
it rise near to the sky-deep.
              There they take
brushingly – with hundred-bird elations –
and
     in a mock sowing (of shadings)
         shake
the aspenwhisper surface of this lake.

1964

WONDERS OF THE SHORE

       It would be fun to own
a collection of senior civil servants
               pebble
   men
     sharp chips worn smooth
             in strange
forms that seem to have earned a kind of knobble
movement
       dry
         waterily the grain
        shown

1965

ROOM

Free from men   Deep country found To hear
the land's voices.   Only the whole music,
ocean-own, of a dale.
                And soon   ears
skilled by that full softness   sift clear
the leaves and grasses from the waters, near
waters from far, far waters from the echoes,
from beck-voices which rock-faces revolve
(some delving falls divined only by echoes);
and closely afresh sift, as windwaves veer
and swell, swirl and settle, making the full
surf of the leaves first conceal then reveal
sighs of grass, talk of a beck over rock,
and these first veil then unveil a low, level
burden like in a shell the sea – the whole valley
by a far rock mirror cupped – which comes distinct
for an instant, together with the tinkle
of a near spring unheard till now and soon
drowned again.
            And begin afresh.
                And so on –
To follow, lose oneself finding and losing,
        through a dale of music,
a skeined music, of masking and unmasking.

*

Spring comes into the city, and the sun
brings out the road-drill. One is down in din
cupped under brick and concrete antihorizon
beside the sediment of a thousand fogs.

Compound corrosion
soaks in,
it acidlogs
tissues and mind.

City of choices –
        one is free in man –
temptations meaning life – good because many:
    town a dale
                where the becks fall
    free – many – and like birds call
telling
        the joy of jostling, the buffer shocks
when they knock up against rocks in a crush
of ripples tripping, the sprint and fishsway wash
down the found channel – as they breathe they freshen
the near air. The hollows fill and bewilder
with dashing counterpoint – egoes and echoes –
all sorts – it takes a town to make a world –
each free to be different and not lonely:
cosmopolis of chances, sacred choices.
To hear, explore, the spirals of the voices,
the skeined score of a city: the intertwining
lives drawing back, comparing, recombining
and disengaging, on and on, if only –

As long as room remains for disentwining.

Until there's no room for any untwining:

    Becks stilled, dales drowned –
    the towned world cannot afford
    valleyfuls of waterfalls.
    From threat of thirst and the power cut
    dams defend the human glut . . .

                    ★

The road out to the dale –
tree-warm windings . . . But here cement-works – dully
pouring across, spreading, failing to rise,
    this off-white dirt cloud.   How do trees
breathe through dust?   Can the green under grey
        still   eat   day?

    Upstream   Find
    the dalehead   Follow
the long dale   in   back under the hollowed
            hills of birth
            (bone structure earth).
Now no road – this young rhetoric of rapids.   It too will
dwindle up – into many.   Now up any
sharp miniworld-of-falls runnel . . . until,
reaching the lip of origin, the mind
    vanishes on into the hill:
        enters the deep fell –
    dark labyrinth the heavens fill
and re-fill – an upheld, hundred-branched well.

The mind diving upspring has left outside
        – here, at this point of birth
(a cryless birth of water from an earth
lip lisping, slipping over into light) –
one's body.   It   climbs on. Then the slope
unsteepens slowly, as the upper dale opens
imperceptibly –
        is the dale-head.
                Wide
and private, the riding sky-sculptured fells' world.

Five senses busy being purified
by lungful after lungful of mere air.
So busy breathing what no man has breathed,

at first all five can only savour
the heady taste, the rare
flavour.   Honey and nothing . . .

Then afresh the cleaned, nimbled eyes take hold.
High
place –
limestone reefs and the shepherds' long
walls every way and, between grey,
free as far as sight,   green –
sweet running grass deserving to uphold
(Amazon, so, the stone sustains the sculptor)
the whole
dome –
the field of the moving fresco, the white
forms with the grey pouches – grave
and light, they leave
way:
the blue   ground of height . . .

When did the mind steal back, to share
the spacing out and newfoundair
(not, not yet quite foul it with forecast – the un-
day of the overcast,   the high place floe-dun,
the cloud   one)?
Simply, now, the white
of flying water letting blue be seen:
the opening order, ray-allowing
conascension dropping play
– shadows and large bright –
to foam of limestone and freedoms of green.
LET THERE BE BETWEEN . . .

Breathed clear in turn, the ear works to unfold
– through a horizonful of the pure music –
ledges, bent holes, ragged edges

of gripping outcrop and willed walls
humming, warbling, and the swirled sigh
of miles of moorgrass next the sky.
What do the sighs of the upland overlay?
Not the spun voices, the twined undertone,
of many waters going down.
Here – when the wind has made sudden wide way –

silence,
one.

*

Sighs   swirl,   masking.
Suddenly the mind
jumps up, and the ears are deaf, the eyes blind –

(day a dark: the open in:
Mandin doing its level dead)

– to all except the mass
of conscience: close remorse;
repentance, urgent yearning to offer rescue,
absurd, at least then give a hearing: face
– still, in the prisons of each other, persons –
wronged posterity. The encircling presence
of spectre futures, the clutching tho' intangible
reproach
of
generations unavengeable –

There is a message to be sent
to you, against whom we have sinned.

1955 - 1975

Calling all individuals, now and –
    (stooping cloud – a stumbling wind)

        *

Calling all individuals!   I call out
– individual in the choking future,
privacy living with the human fall-out! –
to you: call out with love, and stretch out futile
shame towards the cement cloud where you live.
          I have
              to give
      to you – never alone and lonely –
      the poor fact of my foresight only.

With wonder, for it is as if an answer –
(did I have in me, could I transmit, some
pulse,   carrier-wave to bridge time?   or simply
hold a vacuum of attention, such
          that it can suck
          cries from the future?)
– come between the blunders of the wind.
Word comes.   A poem, four-dimensional
intercom of the individual.

I'd given up expecting you to call . . .
Is your previsionary sympathy
pure (are you quite sure?) from hypocrisy?
How much have you foreseen? Did you foresee
my idiot children clustering at my knee
(I mean the ghosts of)? Did you know: we kill
our deformed children (teeming - dominant - from
our gonads shot mad by your radiant litter,
the mutilant mutations; our need of room

extreme)? More ours is it, or yours the guilt
of the infanticides of a long future?
You did foresee it. You know what you do:
know that there will be victims, but not who.
When dead, you still bombard my genital . . .
Never mind, it was kind to call at all.

No sigh: deserted.   Unopposed, the cool
voice, having paused, appears to have imposed
a silence dead different from that holy
serene hovering over open hills:
an irony silence across time,
not good with music which it parts or follows,
but cruel although empty.   The Last Ice,
inert, having rolled as far as could,
occluding all.   The thought: Entropy is God! –

You find me, the nasal plaint resumes, *cool?*
My tone, yes: discipline! – necessity
here, in the stuffy world (your legacy).
It is hot here, the fug of multitude
makes effort incommodious and rude.
The human fall-out, also, you foresee
and use, although you know it leads to me –
you, still proud of inventing ways to grow
more food and fence disease in, though you know
that more will live to starve, more live to die
stunted, die too late, in ourselves our sty.
More mouths, so markets; waste, so markets;   wages
kept up, the illusion that you are of use.
Put off, the drowning dry deluge, to us.
Not riotously even, casually
you waste the substance, the last golden age ...
Rage in me?   sign of life?   Yes.   Totally
futile anger the perfect symbol of
what you to us are handing down as life.

Reading one of your cookery books (illegal)
over a meal of algae, it is hard
not to give way to a heating fit of hate . . .
                    I must keep still.

It stops again.   The silence which those words
have charactered is, again, even worse
than the words, the sad words and unsaid curse:
it rings false, as it fills with of all feelings
the emptiest – pity for victims whom
ourselves doom and will scarcely cease to doom.

Ah!   the wind rises, wide respite.   The surf!
tumbling grass!   quite loud!   sustained! . . . yet too soft!
– a cry drills through: *I will the veils aside!*

In the middle of the infected silence

> *If one might think there is a God*
> *though plainly evil strong Who could*
> *do what one prays*
>   *even reverse*
>   *time's course*
> *to reach back at you with my curse –*
>   *this*
>   *curse –*

>   *To be like us*

> *Prodigal ancestor of us*
> *excess lives   I would sacrifice*
> *room even   solitude*
> *freedom (dreamed still though not had)*
> *to reach and crowd you with this curse*

>   *Be now like us*

Stuck with Man, engaged against one's will
on all sides: submerged, rubbed, in this viscosity
element of intractable waste

— living ivory tower, a person still.
      Inside the blight. There is one cloud
        — no gliding apart, no glimpses allowed —
           and this worldwide;
no contour, play, leverage, way, scope
— no escape: the one climate, too much Man,
descending on the young superb species Mind.

        Observe my fate:
        I live too late.

      Sessile, mainly. Immured in Man.
        One movement free: turn-over —
    error births to still terror deaths.
    Living, buried: dead, burned.
Out on the limb of being buried alive
    long buried still alive
it is dark here because never not light
    never safely private
never getting out of each other's light
or rather (us making the world dark) night —
staring and blind
        still one's mind gropes and clings
with fingers bleeding from the braille of things ...
    and
        eardrums drumming funereal
   drumming
      crowd-muffled
          drowning-loud . . .
    Glued in the glut,
    we live too late.

'Choose' and 'give' – golden-age privileges –
vestiges . . .
Art, maker of room, creator
of open and communion –
even the space of art caved in
under number:
number coating, soaking-down each keen feature:
number pox in the walls, in air – at home
in us the meanness sameness.
The blight inside ...

★

Was that – Did you cry out?   Part of this curse
packs home, truly?   The presence of the future?
the immuring malediction
the feelings of one's victims?
your own remote-control crimes turned on you?
The presence of the future
punishes also me. The problems you
evade and swell – we solve bits, they get worse:
you leave us guilt too.
In the closed circuit brain finely tuned in on
the closed circuit world one hears (again
dismissed in vain)
OUR wronged posterity, this even din
of muted accusation: 'We live under
what we live on, take turns to view the sky,
which less and less often come by.
All light is artificial now, day most.'
      Worse
              then worse
                    unless
Man, built-in warhead, critically massed - - ?

Dustbowl father,   *there still?*
Right.   *I shall try to unravel*
– how can my trapped thoughts make it real
to you in Eden? –
                       the worse evil.
The best, corrupted, is the worst –
        the worst is life debased,
  sacred once,   *now too many:*
slump, market value of life a galloping minus.

Our children (those that are born straight, born sane,
let live) nearly always too close but one's own –
love, yes, will rise still. But like us crammed back
goes bad. Where most the dear is cheap, what good

(tell me, you) can one wish, let alone will
to . . . a drug on the market whom one would
love?
       To a treasure child in a glut world:
       Darling add your mite
       – one life –
            to the surplus.

       Infallibly, though tinily
       ('I must be, I displace')
       you too shall help bring down
       the price of everyone.

       So, sweet, take discreet
       delight in the long service.
       They also serve who only
       stand in each other's light . . .

Bad God, Who set hoping humanity
to silt a world and seep to entropy!

this cruel thing I'm asking You to do
is relatively small, child's play to You,
Illmighty, Woe-efficient!   Merely I plead:
>*Employ omnipotence to implode*
>*in on the squanderers of Earth*
>>*the maim they cause . . .*

If You exist do this at least If no . . .

>*Word without aid! the mere fierce*
>*fact of me human still – no force*
>*except this to beam back in focus*
>*the maim they cause*

>*Crush – no Restrict them quick   with the*
>*thick curse   Debase   Smother with*
>*the fogdreg ghosts of the idiot children*

>*and   (no ghosts alas) the born sane*
>*in vain –*

Choked.   At last.   On a moan.   Poor sweating fool
(not that you curse in vain, O yes I stifle),
get back that breath in the fouled world! shout on! stack
your fending curses
>>against
>>>this I feel
coming – this, the most ill silence of all.
Not even Nothing pure.   The final level
also polluted by the human fall.

★

Instead, these
sighs – grass –
Can a breeze
like a child bringing flowers bestow relief?
What it dips to, touches, is a heaving oval
– a chafe of verdures – dithering past.
Out there, is it?
only?
Here   breathes
to every single blade and feather
thanksgiving for
the unmerited visit,
the blessing of the sighing – though too brief
and the next interval sure to unveil . . .

*

The overlapping, slipping
sighs
cease –
but not the blessing.
They uncurtain a living peace
in which –

the same voice?   this?
One with the justice-mercy rhythm
and Man's pride of irrequiem –

*In old cloud – in the world crowd – on built-down
stream – buried earth long dead – place under town,
even now – if
one listens long enough hard enough often*

the upper dale forms in oneself.

Access! – swirled gaps – to the undertone
  where faint clinks of a near-by spring
  and beck echoes (that far roar) sing
some glory even in the running down.

  Traffic stuck – where could move who?
  but the fire-engine has slid through.

    And dern and grand – though rarely,
still –   *in some among us – the mind and soul*
open out to dalehead.
    The wind-long
selves, the upheld *holding fells –* *high*
  place *fit for a whole*
sky. There are separate clouds. *They shed light,*
and move – a disclosing of clouds kindling
  to white light at the blue of height
   they loose between. *Here*
the listening in some of us

     sifts clear

   silence –

    from in us fairway –

  (clouds   several with holes of height)

Across   time   this   silence Soon
din – continuous But – once discerned –
the unseizing music at a held breath unmasking
  first-fall waters
     space of silence
  is need
    in every head
that will not bury itself till be dead.

  I am I. *I make* *a deep*
of country, in me, and *give what I keep.*

We the too many therefore doomed
have some of us defied our multitude –
　　　grown, wild green, a new virtue from
stifling and inner silt: granting, have room.

　　　No mere limb - room to live was lost,
pain from it still felt. Regained! – gropingly used –

　　　There is between.　　Communication,
earned joy of fraternal confrontation
　　　across the glut of us.　　In us
silence made good by music: antinoise.

　　　My neighbour as if rare
　　　　　　　　　　　　My
chosen land I carry
　　　　　　I am I

1966

BEFORE DEPOSITION

for Robert Speaight

The three masts of Skull Hill and their torn sails
　　　fray the sky
　　　　　　　　The restored stillness
insists with the slight hiss of all the stars

1973

GENTLE PEOPLE

Extinguished in a massacre on the Veldt
            gentle people.
                        They hunted
      food   not kicks
                        and then at rest
preened like the ostriches – and the *qui-vive* quagga
            grazed beside them.
The last of them was carrying in his belt
twelve   small   horns   filled with colours.

Do penance at the cave wall of the self
for the hunted Bushmen end of the hunter-painters.

1972

SOCIAL CONTRACT

Respect between us? Two sorts: one, the minimum,
due from each one of us to every human;
                        and
there's the respect that requires to be earned.

I respect you - you were born and will die.
Show me what else I may respect you by.

NOT SINS AND GLOSSES

Don't expect to find me in my poems –

my pure joys yes
                        hard-won barely held
faith   yes   not sins and glosses The contrast
between my art and my life is my pride

        Poems dance for a person
        whose body is absurd –
        mine has let me down too often
And my mind – I have done things I despise

In my art I evade my evasions

I go away and rise above myself

TO CARRY, NOT DROWN

To speak across time into lack of space
            one needs a quiet voice
        not to drown
                        and the ears tuned
to catch
        the quiet voice if in return it
    should
                put out to time
                                    from
my neighbour in the future without room

TO A VANDAL

What do I feel about you? O . . . unenvy
Supposing you had great gifts plus the will
to work hard to the end of a long life, still
you've stripped the world of more than you could ever
            bring it   you'll go out a
failure your life now in advance worthless

Pity?   for you?   at that thought – yes it wells
up but at once shifts
                        to a man whose work
        you unmade
                    and to people in
    a world without what you laid waste

        Contempt? furious of course –
just cancelled by respect for your remorse
            too late nevertheless

Distaste and cool unenvy – nothing else

        Suicide?   should you? why not? At
        least not a calf more would be killed
            for you to eat of.

WHITE OFF WHITE

There is
        white shadow –
                snow hollows rescinded
by snow crests   (the entire sky sallow)

    or when white fills a window
    and frost superimposes
    a trellis of ash roses

THE LANGUAGE

The fear of dying soon now, the worst fear
of growing old first, yet the need to cling,
though Man seem formed in vain, to the still dear
voices, the hope to see and breathe next Spring –
these crowd in, stifling, clouding, deafening . . .
until fear clears to awe, and one is near
the level sill of silence, listening
tuned by music – by men, divine – to hear

thrilling below threshold of whispers, low as
a sigh of spider-silk at dawn (new and
still balancing spaced dew between caught flowers),
the language of the intertwining winds
on high among themselves – all vowels –
Holy Holy Holy – the names with no ends –

1963

WHAT IS LEFT

Never with nothing but the faith-need left!
To be young, to be young, not yet need faith,
faith the need a man feels when belief fails!
Never to have done enough, enough loved.
To live long and die young – to die alive:
having lived facing life, die facing death.

Less hard to meet the unknown eyes of death
than looks of men living on what we left –
lovers' eyes under world crowd still alive
in corpse faces where fouled blood has killed faith:
the puke taste of the kiss of the beloved,
then hate – gaze seeking us, as desire fails.

Faith's world fails, and imagination fails
at men's and women's life after our death.
We are not yet too many to be loved,
there are still opens, there is true air left,
and fields and trees seen and breathed sing a faith.
In this last golden age some are alive.

Alive. What can it mean to be alive
when each life's value, a life's rarity, fails?
Which of us has the face to desire faith
in face of lives nothing but not yet death,
born well in under world crowd and there left
striving, stifled, still to love and be loved –

bad breath puffed in the face of the beloved? . . .
And can it be that, on some now alive,
the sweet stream honesty will have left
– in this last Age of room (before love fails
by numbers), of people who breathe before death –
a gold dust sediment of surprise faith?

Those who lay waste the future forfeit faith.
O some faith let's leave those we should have loved!
Repenting now of Earth after our death,
I must find ways to make doubt keep me alive.
Growing old now. Not long before one fails.
Doubt is my honour and is what is left.

Faith, reward left by doing with faith?
Faith or no, as one fails, rich with the loved,
young while alive, so meet the blank of death.

1.9.1973

HOW IT SEEMS

God
was innocent
And
omnipotent

No
omniscience

Man
is experience

THE TENANT'S STORY

"Come in, stranger, I thought you were a ghost.
What next? . . . but now, in the light, on the threshold,
you're still more like a wraith errant on Earth.
Sit down – you'll have found it a long journey
out to this lonely cottage. Welcome stranger!
Have a drink – your face says you have a thirst."

It is not drink that will appease this thirst.
You were quite right first time. I am a ghost
– but not dead. Enemy and friend. Stranger
and neighbour. Was already near your threshold
– spacewise. Not long, just terrible, the journey
out. Merely out: aim of my life on Earth.

"What is your name? And your home – where on Earth
was it? Can I appease your kind of thirst?" . . .
Please, a drink all the same. That journey –
it's killing, being alive and a ghost.
He drank, ate, sitting not far from the threshold.
I heard him chewing; it made the thing stranger.

I've no name, a long number. You called me "stranger",
treated me as half friend. No-one on Earth
does that . . . Just across the street from your threshold
my home is. There's no street. *As for my thirst –*
I don't come from the past, I am a ghost
from the future. Through time to space I journey.

To a partly spacious Earth I am let journey
to plant a curse, the thirst, in a past stranger.
I realised he saw me as the ghost.
You're childless – though you have helped to sack Earth
you've not spawned us: therefore, half friend, this thirst
tenderly I set for you below the threshold.

He blurred, but made no move to'ard the room's threshold.
I'd be your child.   For still pure air I journey.
When I've breathed it, it hurts.   Always this thirst . . .
I tried hard to say again "Welcome, stranger!"
He – no, she! looked as old as primal Earth:
Helen once, if young.   Helen's deathmask ghost . . .

And then no ghost. An unseen, coming threshold,
to Earth one mining town – ghost to ghost journey.
I   now   no stranger to a fastening thirst.

Sept. 1973

BOG

            Under treacherous
              heather, slime –
    the place where God was gives. Clutching,
        treading the sucking nothing –

O not self-pity!   Grope for grit of shame,
finger-hold foot-hold shame preparing pride!
I will avenge in advance
                          age, the defeat
which is defeated only as defied:
methodical – by the stones in the mud –
grip,
        lever, and
                      heave out to a hard road.

Mudlogged, I made the road. To die on foot.

1964

NOTHING AND YET

for Linda Gutiérrez

Stand away from the mole's safe
crook   estuary arms   and
that propounding of the surf

      Like a wind
      climb horizon
during days unclasped from land
– evenly ascend the world-
gentle curve of the insea wold
and find
           nothing and yet
                be
     (pit of the bowl walled
      round by the slope of level)
at the dome summit, the high sea

         the colour
        of wild clary

        breathfields

sea
        eye-seed
            Christ's eye

1973

TONGUES

for David Pinner

Absolute shadow (as if a long cave licked)
has adarked on my head – yours – I see, each.
A tongue.   A black flame, thorn-thin . . . Well? what
speech
have you and I – unbabelworthy – lacked?

the apocalypse the geiger counter clicked?
the rosary of the lemmings down the beach
(the Black Death stopped short)? . . . Some gospel to reach
– on Earth we sacked – Man in Man, by Man plagued.

Not quite yet crowded out of the good shallow,
one of the lucky in the last golden age
(lucky except in knowing it) I blink
dazzled at
              the half-light
                            of the Dark Ages
seen from the future, from the full dark.   Black
Pentecost Antipentecost tongues shadow

1970

THE MINDS OF THE NEXT MEN

Ashore on the open (light so hard it blinds
or all but), they will breathe air neat
and lose breath in the first cry . . . but repeat
the breath pain, new amphibians, the minds
of the next men: there look and crawl (or die)
while their bodies still cram shallows and smother.
Yet one thing lashing body and mind to each other –
the first cry on Earth was a rebirth cry –

In the world crowd personal dignity! . . .
Though God be dead, prayer is living; Grace
is human;   now no faith, yet piety,
since our time is for adding the rare good
which men learned in the millennia of God
to what God's skull can teach a naked race.

THE OUT OF TOUCH

This morning friend this evening dead
        how will you pass the night?
I shall not warm you through the lead

        Would I if I might?

The loneliness of the last bed
        has occupied the light –
deathtruth gravechills this living head

        and yet not yet Not quite

THE FIRST AGE OF LOVE
(a sermon to oneself)

> *Even in the eyes of all posterity*
> *That wear this world out to the*
> *ending doom.*

          wake Up

      Breathe
          deep

this air of the new age it is the First
    Age of Love   first love at last
       Man   coming of age
      to love   nameless neighbours
my neighbours across time as well as space

world   wide   Troy my past of neighbours
    coalfrond palimpsests the vast
    fallen forests of neighbours

    all the leaves of the living
        falling

more (if any) all posterity   who
    must wear   out to the ending doom
      world   without room

                        *

Aïe!   this air   hurts –
bitterSpring air   hits
inside – Space-Time is real we live there –
Aïe! . . .
the birth cry   love bequeathed
to men and women who'll never have breathed
air not aged by lungs . . . I'll
breathe as deep as I dare –

Breathe and   hail the nameless: *Man! . . . namesake! . . .*

the so   many so   same
each a number not a name –
still hail the number neighbours with
a forced true love – until the *all*
hail   may seem to call by name
living-on-top-of-one-another souls
bound small like the feet of Chinese girls
before the reign of Mao – souls on and under
(stifled and 'live) each other
helping to fill the world as shut and dull as
a revolution's built-in self-betrayal . . .

Namesake! . . .

★

Tears of the eyes of all posterity –
which
(any?)
can I
dry?
Not   never to be forgotten – write
what could be rediscovered with delight

What could be rediscovered with delight –
I think I see eyes of posterity:
 dry – the stare of irony

   May lover' eyes
   in the world crowd
 not
   if ever they read
  words of mine
      recognise
   hypocrisy

   Look into those eyes

     ★

Jeremiads of lemmings with no sea
    living on their swathed wits
loathing their own as now some blacks hate whites –
 the curse silent the eyes say:
Is there a meaner action than to kill
 and not know whom not even look
spray a village depress pull or twist
   the knob
     each man
   behind a mean
order fouling himself for his country or
 giving the order fouling others
remorse is the time taken to shrug off
can you *(tell me) think of anything more*
mean? *well?* *can you?* *I (I think) can:*
Waste *in the last golden age before*
world crowd

All posterity jealous
and pollute
Posterity will smell us
The last
golden age is the First
Age of the Mean   age of men
stealing from children *Love now is to look*

★

Love   now is to feel
forwards remorse until
remorse grows up to will

Love now   is to will
repentance for
the future –
charity to
posterity

We
got here first   used up the best and got
men late for Earth
We
ancien régime out of reach of their vengeance
deserve what they may serve – the Black Death sentence
They
born overmined

Love is to look what we are doing look
the children in the irony-dried eyes
until –
face stifled lovers' limpid hate until

            the eyes
            begin to
            tell

                        *

            Posterity wronged
            is still the giver
            the child we rob
            fills our need
            after dead God
            a cause to live for

But for true need – the soul's needs of robbed children?

Their scorn the solar wind

1970, 1974

PROPHILY

We need no prophets We know what is coming
            but can we live with it?

        with   our victims – those
                        eyes
in the world camp of refugees from us

        It is prophily we need

            (to love ahead

IT SNOWED IN THE NIGHT

for Robert Meagher

A trumpet? No
a blaze
of snow –

we who were born to live   when
God is dead
live in the age   of
God's resurrection if
there's time
if
room
through open men

the break of God across a blaze of snow

1976

THE PARTITION

for Lawrence Pitkethly

Lives would die of ultralight
  but for the floating slight
     veil ozone

and the void which a soul fears
  shuts brainmining ears
     from the roar of the Sun

     Out there
          in us

between selves and life's deadly source
a less than mist   and the abyss

CAROL

Some shepherds roused –
world the same

They drooped   drowsed
No kings came

The maid smiled
lit by the child

COASTAL STRETCH

      as if
   never moving   yet
drifting between these feet adrift and that
   dune-drift horizon nothing new

     dune out of dune   no
         tune
        no note
    the continuing wind's
wavering drone   seen

       one
   drift   on

  dune   in   dune   un-
   done   delible as a life

JUDGEMENT

Stillnesses   never stagnant . . .

The great poems – those ramparts
cleaned by every wind,
tower-studded crowns emptied
of cities –
stand, regnant,
the bare hill ordeal.

EACH

Forked fires, the trees crackle: as each flare-sheaf
is torn free to be tossed
                              caught
                                        hurled
a rumbling shudder runs through the long world.

Autumn has crammed the storm into each leaf.

Each death gives a meaning to all cold.

RESOLUTION

Shall not pretend to believe, nor refuse
the act of faith.   Will, if the facts so force,
admit but not worship a God less good
than the great music.   If there is a God
Who does not fall below the standard given
by men at their strange best creating Heaven –

God is men making music, music making
silence an ear: the tympanum of silence
carved with judgement covers the giving door
      giving into
                        awe,
                              a vaulted
world of worship stained by walls of rainbows,
a still progress in light filtered by icons.

AT THE CRUCIFIXION OF ONE'S HEIRS

Clouds
     of mud
the heads
          wade
sinking
          wake

Under the crumbling storm
the disgusted last gleam
     pries

     reveals
dice eyes
dividing spoils

LEFT
(at Hiroshima, *e.g.*)

The scorched wall still
stands –
     holds erect, pale shadow, a
     man-shape negative

DOME OF OPEN

for William Alfred

Mind – once the axial jewel to a dome
               pulsing with dim
iconography, one mosaic the stars –
               finds, when it stares
outwards now, the speckled open a scrapped
               senseless script,
and knows itself, if that.   Never a note:
               white noise nought.

Minds hushed by music – these make music, raise
               whole lives to praise,
praise until stoic praise earns singing death
               in that held breath
the after music hush, where music lives
               on and gives
meaning to men, Man's meaning to the abyss
               new-domed by this.

WHAT AN UNFAITH WOULD PRAY

To Kate

If I could know there is a Goddess
or   God
                    if to pray meant
        something, I'd pray
                            for
        Earth to be saved from Man

        And for this "I"
            which seems   mine?
Not to fear death, and never to desire it

        The first I think I have – don't fear
                dying   nor
                fear I shall fear it
                when (soon) it's near
            although now when I hear
            great music truly played
            I feel a twinge of fear
                    (it's late –
                this   the last?)
            listen better than ever

        I have the second too, so far –
            but do
                        fear to live
            maimed, by age and bereavement –
O let me die before I'd rather die! . . .

                    So
                three requests? No:
                one

        Only
be,   O unknown Goodness! . . .

I listen when the music has just closed
Is Someone there it would make sense to offer
      thanks?
        I would
             For
    the divine human
    makers and for
  rejuvenescent fear

Christmas 1975

THE INEFFECTUAL

The fear for one's survivors the love-fear –
    what the now plain and quite near
    future will do to one's young friends
      I find
I do a lot of loving as life ends

1976

II

1976 - 1983

Poet
                    set
Man
                    in
some enaluron of intransigent
                    illumination

so
                    let
the bordure's charge of birds
outsing the howling of our self-damnation

Outsing from 'Outsing the Howling'

CROSS-FADE

Wings of a lark
a twinkling dark
    not long –
    height
fades   shadow to song:
    the voice of light

Heavehover climb
thought against time,
    rage!
    till the hung
throb   dissolves one's age
    to a true tongue

HER FINAL VOYAGE?

    Trendy
    Humanity,
is
  air obsolete?
Earth   out of date –

  windjammer planet?

WHAT DOES MUSIC SAY?

The provocation of great music is:
> some sweet music rebukes.
> Because it is,   says *Why not?*

> > *You heard* it says
> > *Keep faith   Cease*
> > *to acquiesce*

> *Faith   with   Earth!*
> > cries
> music the reminder of
> > love
> > *Praise!*
> > *Praise*
Earth the sense and voice of the Universe –
> > *rare*
> > *tuned held truth*
> > *water and breath!*
> > *Praise*
> > *and spare!*

The fact of music – once known, how deny it?

> > and in the silences
> > still   *You heard* it says

GREY DAY OF THE SOUL

Evil and Good plain

Greed Man in power over Earth the Good
– if I believed in God I should curse God!

Must find if I can
why not to curse Man

NINE PLUS

One rëal thing is   the faith-need:
killed by Church after Church   God
has more lives than a cat

ARE THEY COMING?

It's been a long
drought

Along
the decorated street
souls   dogs' tongues   hanging out

OVER POLAND, 28TH AUGUST 1939

for Anthony Rudolf

Across those wheatfields
                                        which the early sun
is moulding exquisitely
                        dimples run:

(seen from the air) shell-holes of World War One

AFTERLIFE

                Believe?   No.   Half hope

                                For – ?

That those who love
                                meet again whole

                Doesn't one fear?
Hell the remorse looking from beyond death
                at what we did to Earth

YOU WHO AVOID THE ISSUE,

I know I ought not to avoid the issue.
            And why be mealy-mouthed
        and not use the great words
                        when they
            are what I have to say?

Why call a spade and spade and not God God?
    Why talk freely of what a body
                does to a body
        and shrink to speak of souls?

of saving, God-surviving holiness?

            or doom
                    since the issue is
                life and death?

    Why not mention the Universe
                which is where we are living?
Why not call by name and look in the face
                Earth
            Whom we are killing?

TO COMERS AFTER

Posterity of poor!
if   compassion were power
and I could drive this cry through

and past the crumbling babels comfort you

and you in new proud rage
spit on this page

THE NECESSARY EXCEPTION

Whoever has
power for long
shows what he is
and does not see it

sees it wrong
and bends to be it

Exception bring
Man's rarest flower –
hidden king
the pure in power

OWN QUESTION

for Judith Thurman

Horn-hearted as a journalist reporting
            his own question the words
which ripped the dressings off a victim's wounds
the obvious question stridently repeating
          a secret to the winds –

oceankilling oil   forestuprooting
lust   fouled air soil lost
               ask
                  Water!   *woods!*
the Grace of Earth and every love   *parting?*

A man who questions all things is by all
put to the question Mocking racking call
one's own question echoing From what wall?

One is that wall
          And all around is
                I'll
look hard hold my eyes open   to be able
to see with eyes shut what a thing might feel

OPENCAST

for Brenda Rudolf

Clouds   moving off   bright –

now at the shine after the rain
the grass goes deeper into green
and furrowed fields show veins of height

JULY, A STRIDE OF BREEZE

Here come windsteps   blurring
the tops of the trees,   curving
the tips of the straight grasses

– there – there the crops moving
aside   bowing murmuring
as a windfootfall passes

VENERATING SENSES SAVE US

Despair has prevented praise, but praise shall rise again
    beyond despair I will praise here and now

the ordered tones and intervals of the raindrops – how
                      each drop belongs
    to one of the numbered magnitudes (double the last
        and half the next, with none between)

    and praise the reason: droplets descending spin
        some clockwise others widdershins
which opposite revolving   draws together pairs
of drops – but only the equal, which sink at the same pace.
So the liquid lapse is a fabric – the bricks of the rain build
    the First Temple the portal rainbows, one
            for each lifted-up gaze.

            And let no despair
               stop
       praise for the human ear
       staker of music – picking
out of the welter of waves   octaves and simple scales
    and from them forming a pride of rainbows
glancing.
       Man – ear – word
       that builds with the bricks of the
rain!
     Angels tread that ladder, dancing

              *

Rough hexagons are a common
            result of stresses meeting –
            each of the workers swells
            his clamped cell
                                until
– geometry of jostling – the wax froth sets.

Pappas of Alexandria, though, believed that the bees
chose
                        the hexagonal cell   knowing
        this would enclose most honey in least wax,
                and desert Basil (forgetting the stings)
        imagined that the bees were monks and wise.
        Man put beauty into honeycombs,
        religious love gave to the bees its wisdom.

In a froth / in a honeycomb / in a mind
            the outer cells' outward surfaces
            curve   smoothly – the inter-faces
                pack, polyhedral, pointed.
            O seeking senses, locking logic,
            pressing cells pressed to prisms
                to make a mind!   what light
        shall pierce your dark, suffuse your night?
        what light is bright for you to break
    to splinter into splendour as you eat
    to drink its singleness only to pour
            (shattered yet whole and though caught pure)
            out through crystal simplicity
            spectra true to complexities?

★

Angels prefer, for all their wings,
the ladder – the bright bridge that springs
more soaring from
a human dream.
Feet   than fanning feathers far more light
descending! fleet
flames of pentecostal feet
upon the risen silver rungs
between a hushed soul and the singing height!

Chaldean seekers constellated the stars –
which our undoing doubt
shows as one cosmic rout . . .
Age of reverence without
faith – not praying, to praise.

Dextrorse and sinistrorse torsion – weaned and grave
the proportional drops calling their equals as they fall –
affinities of turning love –
the seven terraces, the spectrum, hang in every speck
gardens beckoning . . .
O take –
quick! – your babylon turn,
glad – though the fall be faster the splash at the end little
higher –
to have reflected more of the primal light returning:
refracted it to kind fire.
Bricks like eyes   that eyes on Earth may make
suddenly burn –
courses of colour on high – the thin arch crossing the sky

Make the final silence
a silence after music

1956/1977

DAPPLE ELEMENT

for John and Wendy Trewin

Trailed in the daystream
shadows are eddies

when a wave breaks
it turns a vertical
eddy – trundled on edge

Each
shadow
each caught gleam
is Time made cyclical
– momently complete

Things are coagulated eddies

And lit
stones   grassblades   trees   beasts   clouds

cast
shadow eddies   and
wave-rings of light

A WARMTH OF HONOUR

Stealthy drinker of sea
sun in the cold sky

Warmth from the clear   my
doubt   higher than me

ONE'S COUNTRY

The universe is large: to be eccentric
is to be nothing. It is not   worth
speaking of. (Bronk)

                          Something is worth
the speech of us eccentrics: namely, Earth.

To be Earth patriots
                  is to become not nothing,
Earth being of the Universe not the centre
                  but
                          the sense

THE CURVES OF LIVING

for Kathleen

Cloudy sunny in deep Suffolk
a day of rest
rest from streets   from quadrilaterals
rest   hours   grazing
down lanes between
wildflowerthickets

bulbous hedgerows

trees – spheres lifted

rest for eyes   exercising
loving near and wide
living things   curving

From lattice matter, curves of living!
the poles of the grasses halfway pliant

leaves – lifted eddies

the boles of the trees   led to labyrinth
by histories of the pulls of winds
and pulls of – generations – the sunlust,
green the upward hungers

Above
this
dog-rose hedgerow
an oak round shouldered like a lutanist

SUSPENSION

for George and Mary Oppen

                An evensigh of leaves

            And now across the track there moves
a light baritone din   of sheep's hooves

This evening as though it sealed   world peace –
            evil beautiful / virtue generous:
virile – opposed still –   mazed by a truce

            This air smells as though of the rose
whose petals the Sun dropped
                                Shadows raise
            blue wings
                        as though to fold
            Earth   in Her release

FROM IN EARTH'S SHADOW

Night   black Book of Hours
scattered with small gold flowers

rout of enormous fires
widening nothingness

1976 – 1983

WE HAVE

The scale of the Universe makes sense by proving
                    that size alone is nonsense

                    For finding   holding   giving
                              we have

the scale of values way of life prescribed by
Earth's rarity
                         and the fact of music

WHERE

Backs to the wall?
     this

          is edge –
          the abyss
          touch

Backs to the fall

THE SAINTS

for Carl Rakosi

An animal's corpse smells evil –
animals die against their will.
Leaves dying and dead leaves have a good smell

                    it says that all is well
because the death is their choice – sacrifice
                                    to the tree –
                        life's price
            paid
                    willingly

*

            "It is well that they should die,
            lest they begin to undo
            what they have   so well done.

                    But before they die
            they surrender (. . .) all the residue
                    of their industry
                    that is worth having (. . .)
A gentle current of sugar and more complex things
(. . .) ebbs from the dying leaf into the stem (. . .)

The leaf, useful in dying as well as in living,
                    becomes more and more empty
                    of all but waste (. . .)
                    Across the base
of the leaf-stalk, in a region which is
normally firm and tough, there grows inward
a partition of soft juicy cells, (. . .) a springy

cushion, which either foists the leaf off
or makes the attachment so delicate that
a gust of wind will soon   snap the bridge
            binding the living and the dead."

(J. Arthur Thompson, *The Biology*
of the Seasons. And he added: "This is fine
surgery, that the scar should be ready
                            before
            the operation is performed.")

Sainthood (some report) smells of violets.

*

                        What leaves
                        leave is
                a tree alive

                wood which leaves made
                and leafdeaths saved –

        ancestral leaves not dead
        in wood their dying saved
                – they died and have
                        life in
                their deaths preserved
                        as
tall coaxial channels of saved life
                And the leafmold
                        floods
                        shield
                bulb and seed

*

Deciding the deciduous, wind of ice –
the air visible, tawny! air is leaves!
convulsive – torn off – on the run – which stumble
to plummet yet start up as if the ground

smoked
        and seem hung again bough-high
                                  jigged round
sucked millrace-straight
                  dropped again
                          harrowed
                                humbled

                        ★

The sibilance of the mute mouths of the leaves
shaming us   the preaching of the leaves

those undebasers building wood and breath –
fierce mother leaves – natural suicide –
nearly each leaf a saint and suicide

How holy are the sources of the breath.

                    Greater love
              hath no man than a leaf
            which   to save
      the tree kills itself

mothers to their mother

                      ★

Have I no tree?
What tree but Earth?
Avert Her death!

What can avert it? Only She?

Sometimes I am the tree I see –
I am watching through my leaves
Earth being killed
                              am love which grieves

Mother   shed Your human leaves

★

A wind of the high hills ends
in nets of valley oakwoods, and
stirs
              softly
                        the Fall air full of
the good smell of the suicide of leaves

HER DIRGE

Earth
Beth-
lehem of the Universe

breath
birth-
place of the innocents –

these we take to death

Thee we take to death

COMMONSENSE OF THE SENSES

To perceive is to seek: nostrils clutch
scents, eye-orbs scan, a hand encircles things,
hunger and hunt   race   teeth-palate-tongue,

while the mysterious ears sit still
(never, even in a sleepfast head, shut) –
holding out quietly two shell-like coils
for meanings maybe warnings which the skull's
electric clocks measure as tones like colours.

It is, I know, humanly possible
to love a desert – not all Earth one desert;
to love the Dead Sea – not   every sea dead.
To love a desert, one must know

                                        of leaves
cropping, and that there is a sea with lives.

Young man, young woman, be the Green Apostle

WHILE THERE IS SOIL

     Out walking
                         mind
hoarding trees
               for their approaching
          rarity value

FATHERLESS

A traveller to London caught by night
two hundred years ago rarely saw a light:
dropped into now . . . *"Where? Heaven! . . . Babylon?"*
The ceremonial ways
> *blaze*
>> *on and on*

Showery night, clouds flushed with the diffused
luxury – streets' gold waste notice by few . . .

Along reaches of roofs waterglints tingle –
at windows the dawn is fumbling sand fingers

Men and women of the prodigal cities!
that there is God to forgive terracide is
doubtful   and it's hard to get unkilled

> Look about in the strict light
> Change waste to trees before too late
The death of Earth has now to be unwilled

THE GRAFFITO AT THE FEAST

Moon!
death!

reminder
to deaf
Belshazzar Man
– not also blind –

inspire the
fear of the death of Earth

The repeating graffito hallows
the heavens wall

MAN!

LEARN
TO LOVE:
LIVE
IN FEAR

OF EARTH'S
DEATH
NEAR

TRUE SHARING

Art is
just
the best

on offer
to
whoever
will
aspire
to be its peer

Has to
be earned
Its givers own it
All
who made it
or heard if call
obeyed
relayed it –

who earn it
own it

BECAUSE AND DESPITE

Dante   lyric poet, epic theme –
                with him,
            strung along
the cosmic structure, bloom-clusters of song:

Pound   lyric poet, epic plunge – the Cantos
       shine now and then with Sapphic splinters

THE THING LIGHT

A poem her own lie-detector

      Thingward bound –

         trying
     feigning as corrector
of feignings and,
         the Thing Light found,
      seeing –

poetry is a person being
     simple without lying

PALLADIAN WORLD OF TONE

Music raises façades serene
with interfenestrations of
the plain stone of silence
                         These receive
        all vicissitudes of light
        with variations on their own
               deportment of delight

THE SORT OF PLACE

Moments in the Bible are haunted places –
you come to sudden chill
                         Problem of Evil
no pretence of solving take it or leave it
appears   as a myth   – that is naked

The Holy Innocents
                    Noah drunk   naked
because *the Lord*   *shut him in* in the faces
drowning
            Job's children and their servants take it . . .
And now I feel what sort of place this place is

Here   It   in *us* deep through us snowing
and suddenly we are where we are going –

in   the greed of Man and will not leave it:
have seized all Earth are making Earth too small
to feed all – fouling Her – And we spill soil

We have come to the place It is us   evil

TRUTHTIME

I dread yet hunt truth
to the edge of dread's lying

Am not afraid of dying
Am frightened of death to Earth

VERGE

Soft sounds that fend off silence
yet have   virtue of silence

whispers between kisses
when whispers question
and silence answers
lips mingled
four   lips in a kiss singled

NOBLESSE OBLIGE

Nobly bound to maintain their energy
steadfast at high availability
there is
a selfmade aristocracy –
those who hold off and drive back entropy

IN SOULS' DROUGHT

                poet mind, diviner –
poised on a thumb-ball the divided
hazel twig   waiting to twitch
to some   trickle buried
                        within
                this dust
                this thirst
                this parching
                search

ACCOMPLISHMENT

        I was a child when sea was clean

        We had room I
                        have seen
this earth the sweet rose of the Universe
– during youth I breathed the maiden of air

Soon now I'll die knowing that I have been
Man   fouling to death the One And Fairest

VERWEILE DOCH

The wind has made her hair his own
it darts to catch him
                    he is gone
It droops   now
                and dreams alone –
       no, look!   Again –

GALLANTRY BOWER
(Devon)

The gentle rise
                breaks – here we halt
                      above
the stepping sea the shuffling of the surf –
look down into the February wind
           that's bent up by the cliff –

three yards from the edge
               sit
                 feeling the Sun
      and breathing warm grass scent
     and hearing now and then the sound

OBLATION

Heather, peat, rock

    In a safe crook
           the tarn

          brown
    heifer eye

deepens a blue of sky

COMPANY

"Fear God" says Hermes Trismegistos "God
is a man's natural strength, and company
to the lonely   whoever he be" Indeed
fear: God is the loneliness of the lonely –

God is what drops a man when he is lonely
the grey day of the soul is at last God:
           one is alive and dead,
among the stars Man killing Earth – that only . . .

          Suddenly maybe meeting
true eyes – a visage creased by love – a self
whole: heart of grace keeping body and soul,
          even to the most thin
capillaries of the mind, holily beating . . .

the circulation of the light within

WILL

The flame stands up
                              stands almost still
        not free and yet freestanding
a standing stone of flame
                                    implying

fire-sarsen henges of free wills –
half-transparent poles with standards
        up-held and while held flying

CON AMORE

                          Love

                carved

the baboon of Ripon choir – love, carved

THE FRUIT OF THE FRUIT

The first lie hissed from the ore tree –
                the fruit

                was not
knowledge of good and evil: the gift of Eve is
the good and the evil of   knowledge except
of good and evil

                So
                Eden
lost for – ? original temptation even
                not true?

                Or
                (hindsight if that)
                the wrong fruit
                kindly forbidden

                for
            evil of knowledge has
            taught us at late last
what is   good and what is   evil Now
            we bloody know

LET US PRAY MAN

Calabria '78, a jotting:
An Italian hill city
now has below it several glittery
screes of trash.

The glitter of the litter
fracturefresh
the cachinnation of the jettisoning:
the irreversible frivolous sinning –
Man wasting Earth
in heartless mirth
Blasphemy Man building
Earth's obsolescence in . . .
"God made Man in His image" God is greed?

Trust in the mercy of Greed! let us pray *Greed*
have mercy on us! Have mercy on Earth, O Greed!

We are in greed's Hand
Let us pray Man – we have to

1976 – 1983

SENSELESS

i.m. M. K.

The suicide
let the black star
take his future

Earth has bred
– on Herself fed
the terracide

THE WALK

A clear of evening
has come
– the calm,
the walk home

O twilight   tall sails swift without wind
you make

the walk
guide   as if beside a lake
toward

a slender stalk and level bloom of smoke

as if there were a hope

THE HOME QUESTION

> The woman I love believes
in God – when I
>> seem to blaspheme
>>> she grieves
>> O love! if I as if blaspheme
I worship though I may not yet believe

Only those who will tell home-truths to God
> honour the pride of God
I'll not insult God – behaving as if
God were afraid to face the problem of Evil

Suppose an Almighty unworthy of
> men's best – I'd scorn   Him
but if there is a Lord Whose will is love
I must be frank with Him just as I am
> with my wife whom I love

Is it God's will to let Man's greed end Life?

IT WAS TIME TO BE SKINNED

Shrinks at the thought of a touch
– or of reclining
                    afraid
        to rest   most

Any breeze a fresh torture

A person has been flayed
        by a ghost

            of someone future

AS NEAR AS I DARE

The want, haunting –
                    again consent to wait –
            conditional guardian angel
                    to live
                    with
            subtle danger
            everywhere.

As near to wishful thinking as I dare
I take the consequence of music; give
the act of faith to music – take its word
            and hear
                        pure the faith
which must be earned by doubting until death

WHEN SHE IS DEAD

The coming death of Earth
does not invalidate
dolphins   leaves   leafbreath
music's act of faith –

Earth's coming death
invalidates God –
brute
       quantity
of hydrogen and distance
shrunk
       by quality
having had existence

Earth's final silence is a curse
   which drowns the Universe –
       good
     outroars the stars

Chirp of dolphin
         rustle of leaf
   surf of life
       music's
  hush –
     O could
the sweet roar
overtake
    make
every star an ear of God

VOCATION RAPIDS

There is perhaps no God but there are things,
people, times, that are holy – the washed king's
awakening to kneel to his wronged daughter –
cave-walls charged with the light of men encircled
by absolute   dark – and this
                              this work
laid on us by freedom
                    to make men human
at last and virtues (bright forms) hold. O duty
crown!   thorn burning   never consumed!

At a discovery a man's mind stalls:
his full stream crammed back into sudden dalles,
he gathers, in his cloudchamber brain plotting
antics of thought whose waves against the pierced
                screen of his interposed
doubt   break into particles – paths splitting

WRAPPED

After music
              we may go
through streets and tunnels, carrying
silences of offering –

        green shot with indigo
        the drake's-head afterglow
of music
              scarfs us where we go

III

1984 - 1990

To face the fall of all gives no protection
from resurrection –
life is to rise again until we die

not know   try
protected for exposure
in despairing
sow   new daring

The Common Resurrection from 'The Fact of Music'

SHOCK

To the vulgar boastings of the Lord to Job
the now fully forlorn retort a jibe:
               not save
               this loving
               Earth
               from death?

A man who made his child learn being free
        would not sit by and see
           the child
        kill all and killed
  but God   would?   it is His nature –
a too faithful so unfaithful Creator?

Earth plaguespot spinning on – dead, active – foully
soaked in the halflife of Man's festering lilies?
        good?

    (I am a man shocked by God)

MAN HAS BEEN HOLY

"If there is God we do not know
the only word for God is 'O'"
from 'O'

I thought of Chartres Cathedral and again found it
a praise nobler than God

                  and men made it
       And God wills other men to end it?

In spite of the disgusting likelihood
we need to find there's a non-vandal God
           – know
an unnameable Earthcherishing Good

        O!
        become!
        be come!

HEAR OUR PRAYER

"If   I grow up"
               said a poet's
son – thirteen –
           grown and not know it

God! if You are and hear, give youth
to children aged by the nuclear truth

DEFY THE CREEPING HELL

    The slaves of the mills and mines went
          first:
                in the end
          us all
– things green – fishes beasts birds mankind –
          contaminands

    But I'll defy the creeping Hell:
          have heard –
          made
the irreversible acquaintance of
glory: I unbelieve, and yet receive –
          shall   listen and give

A MAKING OF PLAINS

Crowds – frothfickle gift
in the imitative cities

In a cell is a street in a grid
a self a grid of greeds

    Guilt-quags sink –
    to plains of silt
humanity interdegrades

TAKEN

Agnosticism - vow of poverty

Franciscans in Great Britain (my wife tells me)
        have this custom: often one
is sent out for six months into the world
        by himself – no money,   only
                the clothes he's in

    no destination – God will guide him

They say it always works   For them it works

        We are agnostics now:
                to dare to see
        is to take this vow
                of poverty

        Sight sends us out
        alone with doubt:
    each of us – each time we dare –
    walks with nothing into what's there

        There seems to be no God –
A Goddess in mortal danger is our guide

                It works for us

        For we are Hers
        and there is grace
        in this doomed Place

THE STORM

The sea is beating up the wrecked
ship –   goes on and on   hacking
gouging
            twisting
                        and again   hacking –
tearing even after breaking –

                  no! it's the storm's
savagery has savaged savage
        the sea, which owned few harms

Look how mankind – greed unconfined
(except by the greeds intergrinding) –
is heaping up self-triggered ravage
            till it transforms
        all inviolate things
trees   grasses   stones   springs

to raped furies forced to collide,
share humanity's suicide

THE SHIVERING SOUL

Theology is an art – of codifying
wishful thinking: between transparent flying
buttresses of a logic that aspires,
the labour of theology – elegant – linking
aloft teetering vaults of wishful thinking . . .

gospel beyond gospel the telescopes
peel the palimpsest heavens – the scraped hopes
dissolve to the one wilderness of fool's fires:
nearly every edifice-belief has
a base no less diffuse than the Universe

The secrecy of the shivering soul shimmers
as the gleams foam in her mind's hall of mirrors

The swimming gallantry – vessel pinnacles spires –
tilts, sinks
                    Soul gropes alone
                                        In the arms of dying
Earth she finds herself held, healed by defying

FIGHTING THEM OFF

The stars the far and dead
    press on my head –
their points burn in a sphere
    prison-near
To give the vault of night
    volume height
       I fight

      find
the suction of the stars
    prising out mind:

in the draught of the mere
expense,   of fusion fires,
thought   catches fear
   from their flight

    I
    defy
abject stars with the rare
    here

MOMENTARY

The arch of colours – huge – joins . . .

Just within it a strip shines
already in sun – of the green plain

seen through a thin muslin of rain
against whose grey a few gulls gleam

stabs of white – stars in a dream

TO THE FOREHEAD EDGE

I *comb grey hair* – my soul is brown
              The hair
        receded long ago
Thick, to the forehead edge my soul is growing

    poetry   youth in old age

    love of Earth   a pure rage

YEAR IN

Robed and rhythmic ritual –
re-enacted mystery –
year: Eve's re-nativity
leads   again innocent into
fair-limbed summer's serpent snare

Soon at the gate of every tree
autumn's expelling angels flare
till cold has killed the will to enter

     The blades fall
     It is keening winter
   Adam's funeral

(?1952)

MEDICINABLE WORKS

Soon or late or both   a man's alone
     with a despair too true to pass

unless
     into that desert of his own
        honesty
             there come
a tangible thing – human yet good   some
     soil-heal action
             or some
     companionable masterpiece
     made from an earlier loneliness

TO BE USED IN CHURCHES?

O mysterious God, Who did, among the billions of billions
of flaring stars in the wilderness of galaxies, find place for Earth,
a temperate speck allowing water to flow, air to clear
and life to grow, to try many varying forms, among them
mankind,
bodies weak and vulnerable but thoughts which have
gained the power to conquer and subject Earth to Man's greed,
mankind now using this power to plunder and poison the
planet
and competing to make and stock weapons which may at
any time horribly destroy all life on Earth,
O mysterious God,
hear our prayer:

Save us even now from the evil of irrevocable knowledge, by
guiding it to bring forth lucid prudence,
bring forth in us the wisdom to avoid the nuclear massacre,
and to defend sea and soil, air, ozone, plankton, grass, trees
and springs
against rapacity and fecklessness;
O mysterious God,
make the extreme danger (here and now, and always present
from now on) cause in us love for our neighbour in time as well
as in space,
love for the people who share Earth now, and for those who
will share what is left.
Amen.

A FLAVOUR BEHIND LIGHT

for Judith Thurman

I have tasted the dark of a long cave
darker than any night – dark as a grave . . .
I taste
          the end of eyes –
                              the Sun unseen
the starry skies unsearched: in back of green
chestnut-crowns eating light that's building trees
and grass-blades sipping light which sight still sees,
the death of Earth is there
                              Earth here still, gleam
riding this clear-stem fountain's top of bloom

Sun – breeze – the gardens playing in the rays of
fountains – light-fingered fountains – flowing fingers
sifting with harp-glissando laughter the maze of a
cedar, where glows from one bough's blue-green gloom
– tail of jewels drooping – a peacock sleeping

I have tasted the dark the taste   lingers

WRITHING START OF END

From in   the hardofhearing stratosphere
        subSuns scything a hemisphere
                        naked   blind

a writhing halfworld of flayed eyeless fauna
        – patches left behind
        to curse a halflife era

        No trumpet-call could breach
the wall of poisonous disatmosphere
nimble with toing-froing rays of itch
– steep, tall, deep-founded
                        between each and each
        still clutching creature

SHE, STILL

Night   has wept big
                        and now
        the unveiling of the dew . . .

        She   still!
        – Earth   in
        the awe of morning

        Un-
        moving
the stemmed dewbearers - each green grail

ON OUR OWN

for Julia Farrer

It may not even matter whether
      the whole makes sense or none
What matters is to make one's own
             life a meaning

A life makes sense with other lives
    together
           mother father
brothers & sisters
           strangers children
    animals   trees   vines
           air
           the waters

Seeking the precinct of one's life,
focus beauty in to truth:
through interplay with lives and Earth
make   a life good in itself

      Earth Mayflower

GRACE ITSELF

The idiot beauty of a violent poodle . . .
over and over the broad lawn a poodle
                chasing shadows of flight . . .

A grace of waste – no purpose except life

HEARTH EASE

Feline flames

      ember
      elves

washing themselves

AN EVENWHILE

Hand over fist the trees climbing the hill

      Let us
              at the stream
                        still
          an evenwhile
       tread   a loam of leaves
and read the eyelid-coloured clouds

QUANTA SABBATH

If one threw a pair of dice
ten hundred times, the 7 would win:
one thing's for certain – likeliness
            though meaningless

        from star blaze
        to quark point
            no mind
            no hand
moronic moonings zombie God

        Soon Earth will spin
        lifeless   in
fields of shifting lifelessness –
        no God, but dice

Still perhaps (rare, remote) a run
of 2s and 12s   may be thrown
            – and poise
        an Earth of lives again?
One thing is certain – likelihood:
the universal waves-jig governed
by   the dice cast by disGod

        till on is gone –
            no mind
            no hand:
        throwing alone

THE CERTAINTY PRINCIPLE

Walking the sheen of the river
my freed gaze is a breeze
touches and to a shiver
dishevels what it sees

Telescopes   synchrotrons
noting throws of dice
– God   over there once
but could not cross   twice

quarks   stars   vanish
into field   through vast:
while eyes and ears live, values
are the selves which last –

beauty goodness truth
in things and lives, revealers
of humble divine Earth –

Whom   let's not abolish

ON ONE'S SLEEVE

It's hard, now, not to wear the abyss on one's sleeve
From waste that makes us nonsense, what is left?

Virginal, open, the air on Hadrian's Wall,
secret as Lundy!
                    for how long? Meanwhile
the world's not yet treeless Down here a breeze
                    A field with two oaks
                    at gaze – the judge trees
creaks   crackle a joke   wag their wigs
Among 'live rocks life-giving water talks . . .
The tiercerons and liernes of each leaf!

Haydn's apple music makes the Sun rise:
let there be light – when he writes it, there is

                    Either the Bomb – or the
breath of Earth, Mother, Man-smothered
                    – either way
the waters the leaves each promise, all all lives,
the species of Earth's progeny of loves
all all potential loves in advance withered –
we are too many our waste drowning Life's self

It's hard, now, not to wear the abyss on one's sleeve

27 - 31.xi.82

TO ONESELF AT A ROADSIDE

Know your self – that it is a servile thieving
beggar with braggart sores and you've been living
under lucrative ulcers of your sin
                    yes   it's your   skin
you a deformed informer warm within

Know it by not going past on the other side

Achieve   even to yourself   charity:
wipe the pus from the wounds draining its pride –
cure it of cadging off successors – of leaving
them   treeless
                        to breath your filths   in . . .

That self (yours) left for dead will live   when
neighbours-to-come find robber turned Samaritan

EITHER . . . OR . . .

The self-blinding
a soul lying –
the sin against the light –
as if a poet lied

★

The span of listening – the silently
burning authority: woman or man
diffident,
awed wide
when
to hear could be to see
and catch the unseen hand

SHIP-SHAPE, SOUL-SIZE

Stand in dry-dock, gaze up the overhanging
side of one's curving soul careened for scouring
– small below it
my boat soul –

and yet, to launch, load, sail,
I own her!
sturdy   watertight   steerable

may drown me

IN LETHE LIGHT

Seen from Earth's shadow, the black sky has some
light   either from the peripatetic
angel of Alldeath the dead Moon, or from
the God-faint choir of dead angels the foam-
of-fire Lethe, torrent of holocausts . . .

of which this circling darkhouse – while she casts
the beam, Space-raker eyes – can unveil part . . .
Lethelight: shadow-hooded sight, interpret!

We   alone? being shown the Abyss Stream
– manyness – sheer: meaningless
                              So? . . . We seem
to be   Meaning: bring to the stars Meaning –

fluke Life the sense and glory of Phlegethon-Lethe!
pools,   memory . . .
                        Mere good, stern greed!
Day   each day desperate sanity

WHY EVEN A DICER?

Zombie machine-gunner
Everspray of shot

    all
    sizes –
rapids of holocausts
fall   black holes
    also the
    infra-
infinitesimal
    surprises
(nothings that ricochet

Ammunition   endless
Fingertrigger   mindless

LUCIFER'S-EYE VIEW

There's EARTH!
    derelict-hull . . .

      spinning on
    with the bones of Her crew
    mutinous Man

    who
looted his home . . .
    Stifled in waste – his own!

    eye   if any
    in after,
    if any

LIGHT-ROT

With its invisible load
of ultra-violet
the gold Sun's light
eats the glazes of paintings –
the canvas may light-rot
(not veiled) to a dispainting

Ambitions slouched to greeds
spend the soil with the green:
soon – Man grown too many –
Earth is a sacked city:
starved peoples beg pity
from the rich caught in famine

KNIFE-EDGE

The Universe, after Earth dies?
Luminaries galore, no eyes

The stars
need eyes
need us
So long as plants can live or eyes
see, there's meaning – none if Earth dies

The Universe was likely, life unlikely:
men lapse to likely – chop all Earth down eagerly

If man makes sense at all
he may make sense of all

NIGHT SKY HISS

Secreted by long minds, antenna shell –
    giant ear-trumpet ear-to-sky
        awash with   the highest
sea's   inviolable surf-soft   hiss

      Hiss of the Universe?
fire-surf breaking on no shore
      except such ears as this?
          In
      ears shielded by Space
          (the vast
          Sparse)
      a thinned-by-distance din
      of roars of holocausts?

          Soon
        none to hear
          stars
          roar:
        the Universe
        less than a hiss

REAPPRAISALS

The 'plane's port engine had caught fire
    copper-bright – hot
to one's face – I watched – found myself cool
"So this is it . . . I suppose it will
       hurt
       but be short" –
and when the blaze went out and one propeller
dropped away   it was a good   thought
that in the coming war I'd at least not
      look a fool
      by showing fear.
So, 46 years back, my death seemed near

21 years back, dying began to feel
statistically likely to be near:
      wrote then *Concern with Death* [1] –
spent the next years more living than half-living,
      at Christmas '75 could say
      what an unfaith would pray [2]

    But now? Am I afraid of dying?
      Kept just not dead – of that
        perish the thought!
        But dying? –

      to be replaced
      because surpassed
    as petals follow sepals
        being
        old
    grow free, not cold

    down in a warmth of trees

die investigating

Every thing one loves   is
precarious – music ends   lives
    vanish. Holiness is
    precarious – not less holy
    Because precarious holy
    and then not there   All
    is to be made new

    Ah   but if   few
    trees   then nowhere trees –
       no sepals waiting

         no breath

      lifeless seas

    Still *not afraid of dying*
    but frightened of death to Earth [3]

1985

1.   *In this Transparent Forest*, pp. 128-131;
2.   *Ibid.* pp.145-146;
3.   *Commonsense of the Senses*, p.40

HIGH ENERGY CONSTRUCT

Free, I will not just run down. Therefore form: a
dam   completing convergent fells, to enfold
a head of water-hill-bowls slowly filled,
a single duct. So the projective rhymer
shall generate a head
                              of reserve dreamer
energy   -
            powering mansense and folly
destruction and fraternity, the field a
radial network – DANGER! 'live lines from a

sonnet, that dynamo, as small and neat as
the contained monster at the cliff dam's foot is
to its rays of cables riding gallops of pylons
with hidden loads of light
                              and of intense
damning dark   greed-mad, the fall-out fountains

sonnet charging souls with high-tension silence

FROM BETWEEN CLAWS

to Pierre Rouve

So one more barefoot ghost shut in an hourglass
                dreams of the claws of eagles?

A man now knows that he no longer stands
                between raised chalicing hands –

            unless it be green hands Earth-raised
            one's length an anthemlength of time
        a poet the precentor
                                of Earth's praises

PIONEERS! COME

                from
the planned, perilous journeys
after receding matter!
                Learn
                to return
– hardy now, and haggard –
                home!

to Things, the virgin country –
Earth virgin in spite of
Man all-corruptive

GREEDWASTE

A city was a tower: is a town
has crumbled to a Babel, has come down
to its own suburbs   people speak just one
language, in ears-to-hear a foreign din:

girls flickering to work in demure morning,
the cornices shining without meaning;
blue, and the Sun, summon the greedwaste demon
and grind . . . endless dust,

                    the famine Amen.

Land after land these strewn skeleton rivers –
all the litter deltas of humanity
abandoned by sweet streams: hands upturned
scrawled with dead languages, spectres of rivers . . .

We sponge on our youngers and betters: every
soul now living is a remittance-man

WHILE HUMANITY STILL . . .

Is Earth the one Divinity
          may have survived
           to face alone
the question without mercy thrown
by what can never be un-
            known?

MAY CHANGE

to Sister Rose Mary C.S.P.

Before Man
over-ran
Earth, there were

hunted hunters
(the fight fair) –
from prey learned
dance in
rock – water air –

cavern-painters

Human nature
changed since then . . .
May change again

HEDGE SAYS

Here again Earth
faces the Sun with a rose

Earth holds the ace of roses
there has been birth

THE EMPEROR

. . . shivering
Man most naked
of us all . . . George Oppen

Yes
     since Man has
no manproof clothing

           the weather
which will kill him is
       his

TYCOON SONG

A low hill
in Brazil:
a loaf of cloud
almost still;

a wonderful
bloom smell
(the good beans
a merchant burns) . . .

Harvest-waste
whole-roast
sweet the smell
of holocaust

THE LOAD

Ingeniously insensitive to how leaden
     irony is
          (with all that lightness) –
poets and critics peeping from a fashion,
     playing for safety, to shirk vision –

          BASTA! I'd lightly
        take the load
and stand clear of the irony evasion

FEAR OF MUSIC

Passion debased to an intrusive background –
       screech of its craving patrons
       busy drowning the clear
dew of life in reach of everybody:
        (in reserve?)
        carried around

      Music
          (the true,
      now feared
          so drowned

1984 – 1990

LIFTED

            Saps
            pressing

            buds
            piercing

        and soon burning
        open-hearted

all the prayers passing
                the earlobes
                the eyelids

of God the beginner learning
        what He started

DRESDENS DISTANCED – NO SAFE DISTANCE

From twelve hundred feet up,
seventeen miles away,
the city is one blaze
sleeping like a top,

not singing – a soft roar
as if bare quantity
of gathered agonies
        hurt no more
and horror's beauty undid
        what it hid

FROM IN

Perhaps   we
(not to see
         know
         now,
after-Man's   end
         all
         trees
         felled
         from in

         soils
         sullied
         seas
         fouled

after-Man's   end
         the sin
         of Man
         deathdealing

         on . . .

TO FRIENDS WHO WILL SURVIVE ME

I live a double life – have to, am two
            diverging: one of me
      has a feast life
                        the longed-for-wife –
my betters' art – myself at latefruit work –
Spring yet again and some still unspoiled walks –
friends – travel – wine (and both of me believe
it's sin not to enjoy blessings we have)
            while the other

recognises this robbed Earth's poison air
      we are bequeathing
                        you to breathe in
and would – my noGod! no! – not live to see
      what we prepare come true

If an agnostic's nearest thing to prayer
has any value
            mine is here for you

1982